Picture the Past

Life in the Dust Bowl

Sally Senzell Isaacs

Heinemann Library
Chicago, Illinois

© 2002 Reed Educational & Professional Publishing
Published by Heinemann Library,
an imprint of Reed Educational & Professional Publishing,
Chicago, IL
Customer Service 888-454-2279
Visit our website at www.heinemannlibrary.com

Produced for Heinemann Library by
   Bender Richardson White.
Editor: Lionel Bender
Designer and Media Conversion: Ben White
Picture Researcher: Cathy Stastny
Production Controller: Kim Richardson

06 05 04 03 02
10 9 8 7 6 5 4 3 2 1

Printed in Hong Kong

Library of Congress Cataloging-in-Publication Data.
Isaacs, Sally Senzell, 1950-
   Life during the Dust Bowl / Sally Senzell Isaacs.
      p. cm. -- (Picture the past)
Includes bibliographical references (p.) and index.
   ISBN 1-58810-248-3 (hb. bdg.)   ISBN 1-58810-413-3 (pbk.
bdg.)
   1. Dust storms--Great Plains--History--20th century--
Juvenile literature. 2. Droughts--Great Plains--History--
20th century--Juvenile literature. 3. Great Plains--Social
life and customs--20th century--Juvenile literature.
4. Farm life--Great Plains--History--20th century--Juvenile
literature. 5. Great Plains--Social conditions--20th
century--Juvenile literature. 6. Depressions--1929--Great
Plains--Juvenile literature. (1. Dust storms--Great Plains.
2. Droughts--Great Plains--History. 3. Depressions--1929.)
I. Title.
   F595 .I83 2001
   978--dc21
                                    2001000500

Special thanks to Mike Carpenter at Heinemann Library
for editorial and design guidance and direction.

Acknowledgments
The producers and publishers are grateful to the follow-
ing for permission to reproduce copyright material:
Corbis Images: Arthur Rothstein, pages 6, 7, 8, 11, 14;
Bettman Archive, pages 13, 22, 23, 26, 27, 28; Bettman
Archive/UPI, page 10; Corbis, pages 12, 19, 21. Library of
Congress: pages 1, 3, 9, 15 (from Franklin D. Roosevelt
Library), 16, 17, 25. Peter Newark's American Pictures:
pages 18, 24, 30.
Cover photograph: Library of Congress/Franklin D.
Roosevelt Library.

Every effort has been made to contact copyright hold-
ers of any material reproduced in this book. Omissions
will be rectified in subsequent printings if notice is given
to the publisher.

Illustrations on pages 20-21 and 29 by John James.
Map by Stefan Chabluk.
Cover make-up: Mike Pilley, Radius.

Note to the Reader
Some words are shown in bold, **like
this.** You can find out what they mean
by looking in the glossary.

ABOUT THIS BOOK

This book tells about the daily life
of farm families who suffered in
America's Dust Bowl from 1931 to
1938. Experts give many reasons
why life became so hard for these
farmers. They say that farmers
ruined the land by planting too
many crops. Also, hard times hit
the rest of the country and people
could not afford to buy the farmers'
vegetables and grains. And then
came the very worst years, with no
rain and strong wind storms.
We have illustrated the book with
photographs taken during the Dust
Bowl days. We have also included
artists' drawings of how people
lived in that time.

The Author
Sally Senzell Isaacs is a professional writer
and editor of nonfiction books for children.
She graduated from Indiana University,
earning a B.S. degree in Education with
majors in American History and Sociology.
For some years, she was the Editorial
Director of Reader's Digest Educational
Division. Sally Senzell Isaacs lives in New
Jersey with her husband and two children.

CONTENTS

The Dust Bowl

"America's Breadbasket!" That is what people have called the farmland in Texas, Oklahoma, Kansas, and Nebraska. Much of the world's wheat is grown there.

But for several years in the 1930s, the wheat did not grow at all. The corn did not grow. Not even the grass grew. During those years, there was no rain. The farm fields turned to dust. Strong winds lifted the dust and blew it everywhere. These dust storms created an area that was called the Dust Bowl.

Look for these
The illustration of a farm boy and girl show you the subject of each double-page story in the book.

The illustration of a farm house highlights panels with facts and figures about everyday life in the Dust Bowl.

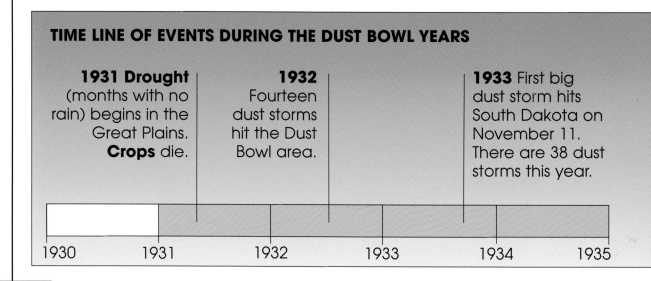

TIME LINE OF EVENTS DURING THE DUST BOWL YEARS

1931 Drought (months with no rain) begins in the Great Plains. **Crops** die.

1932 Fourteen dust storms hit the Dust Bowl area.

1933 First big dust storm hits South Dakota on November 11. There are 38 dust storms this year.

| 1930 | 1931 | 1932 | 1933 | 1934 | 1935 |

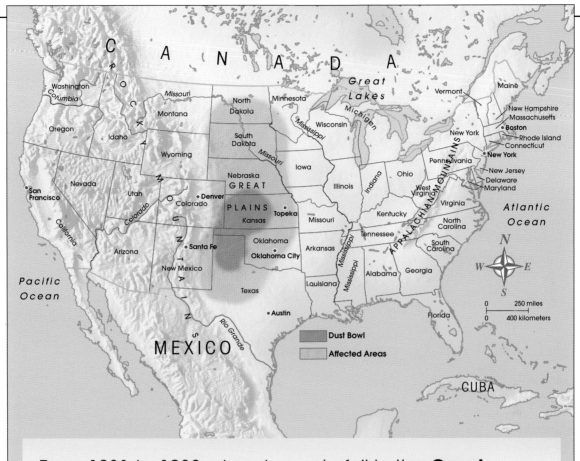

From 1931 to 1938, almost no rain fell in the **Great Plains.** The people in the area known as the Dust Bowl suffered the most. The Dust Bowl included parts of Texas, Oklahoma, Kansas, New Mexico, and Colorado.

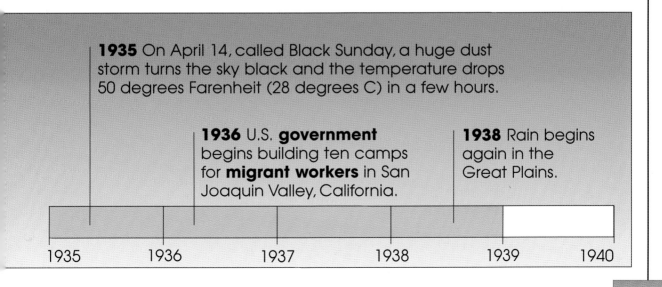

1935 On April 14, called Black Sunday, a huge dust storm turns the sky black and the temperature drops 50 degrees Farenheit (28 degrees C) in a few hours.

1936 U.S. **government** begins building ten camps for **migrant workers** in San Joaquin Valley, California.

1938 Rain begins again in the Great Plains.

| 1935 | 1936 | 1937 | 1938 | 1939 | 1940 |

On the Farm

The farmers' fields seemed to roll on forever. There were thousands of farms, but they were spread far apart on the **Great Plains**. The closest of neighbors lived miles from each other.

Farmers grew wheat, corn, barley, and oats. They raised animals such as cows, pigs, and chickens.

A farmer and his family lived in a wooden house built on the edge of the fields. The farmer built a barn for his animals. Wheat and corn were stored in other wooden buildings.

This farmer is using a horsedrawn **plow.** The plow breaks up the **soil** and gets it ready for planting seeds.

FASTER PLOWING

Starting in the 1920s, some farmers bought the newest kind of plow. It did not need animals to pull it. It was pulled by a tractor with an engine. Tractors made plowing easier and quicker, but they cost hundreds of dollars.

Many of the farmers grew wheat and sold it to **mills.** Machines at the mill turned the wheat into flour for bread, cakes, and noodles. As long as the weather was good, the farmers grew wheat. As long as people bought bread, the farmers made money.

The Farm House

Most farmers were not rich. Their houses were small with just two or three rooms. Many farmers **borrowed** money from banks to pay for their houses. Some farmers also borrowed money to buy seeds, animals, **plows,** and tractors.

This man and woman are proud of their new farm house. They hope to sell enough wheat, chickens, and eggs to pay for it.

By the 1920s, many farmers had trouble paying the banks for the money they borrowed. Many people in other parts of the United States had lost their jobs and did not have enough money to buy food. Many **mills** stopped buying wheat. Farmers stopped earning money.

Most farm houses had running water but no electric lights or telephones. These children are reading in the main room, which was used as a kitchen, dining room, sitting room, and play room.

No Rain at All

In 1931, more trouble arrived. For months and months, there was no rain. The **crops** stopped growing. The **soil** in the fields dried up into dust. Even the grass turned brown. There was nothing for the farm animals to eat, and they began to die.

As the fields dried up and crops died, the farmers searched the sky for rain clouds, but none came.

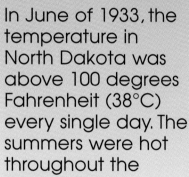

HOT AND DRY

In June of 1933, the temperature in North Dakota was above 100 degrees Fahrenheit (38°C) every single day. The summers were hot throughout the **Great Plains.** People could not waste water on a cool bath or shower.

When there are several months without rain, it is called a **drought**. There had been droughts before the 1930s, and there have been droughts since then. But this one lasted for almost seven years.

This boy's family may need to sell his calf to buy food or to pay for the farm. Children were upset when animals they had grown up with had to be sold.

Black Blizzards

During the worst of the **drought**, the dust storms began. Big gray clouds rolled in. The winds lifted up the dry dirt from the fields and blew it everywhere. The air was black. As people ran home, they could not see their front doors. Sometimes a storm lasted a few hours. Sometimes it lasted a few days.

This Oklahoma farmer sees the dust storm coming. Animals must be rushed into the barn before they get buried by the dust.

Dust blew into eyes and scraped against skin. People ran into their houses. They jammed towels around their doors and windows to try to keep out the dust. But the dust blew in through the tiniest cracks. Parents gave their children wet cloths to put over their faces to keep out the dust. People became sick from breathing in dust.

This picture was taken in Kansas City in March 1935. It is the middle of the day, but the sky looks like night. Even with street lights and car lights, it is hard to see through the dust-filled air.

Digging Out

Dust was everywhere. It covered floors and furniture. It settled inside glasses and cups. All the dishes had to be washed. So did shelves and clothes in closets. It took more than a broom to sweep the floors. Sometimes it took a shovel.

Dust filled and piled up against this **shack,** making it unusable.

With no **crops** to sell, farmers sold their tractors and animals. Soon they would have to sell the house and land and leave the **Great Plains.**

After a storm, farmers went outside and dug out buried tools and fences. Sometimes they had to dig out their cars. Many car motors filled with dirt and stopped working. Farmers had no money to repair them. The storms hurt the animals, too. Farm children spent hours cleaning dust from the noses and ears of cows and pigs.

A Child's Life

Children in the Dust Bowl watched their parents worry about money. But they still went to school and took care of the farm animals. Young children fed the pigs, milked the cows, and collected the eggs. Older children helped their parents out in the fields, herding the animals and driving tractors.

HEADING HOME— BACKWARDS

At the first sight of a dust storm, teachers sent students home. On very windy days, children walked backward so the dust would not scratch their faces.

Children learned to play with anything they could find. These two girls are using **tumbleweed** as a bed for their dolls.

Children played games that did not cost money. They hung a rope from a tree and used it as a swing. They played kickball in the yard or jacks on the front porch.

These children are playing on a merry-go-round made from a wooden wagon wheel.

News and Radio

THE WIZARD OF OZ

In 1939, people loved the movie, *The Wizard of Oz.* It tells the story of a poor girl from a farm in Kansas. A **tornado** blows her away to a magical land.

There were no televisions at this time. Farmers got their news and **entertainment** from newspapers, radios, and movies. Everyone who owned a radio had a favorite radio show. Most shows lasted fifteen minutes. They were funny, scary, and exciting.

With a radio, families could listen to news, stories, music, and sports reports. Radios were much larger than they are today.

Most farmers never saw famous baseball teams, such as the New York Yankees. Thanks to radio, they could listen to each pitch and run of a game. Everyone knew about the "home run king," Babe Ruth.

It costs ten cents to see this movie. For the price, these boys will probably see a movie, cartoon, and **newsreel.**

Packing Up

The rain never came. The fields became dryer. The farmers became poorer. Millions of people packed up and left the Dust Bowl. Some sold their houses and land for low prices. Some just walked away from it all. It was time to look for work and schools someplace else. It was time to breathe fresh air.

This family is leaving their farm. They do not know where they will live next. They are homeless.

Children sadly said goodbye to their teachers and friends. Many of their friends had already left. People had heard about the farms in California. Those farmers needed lots of help. It sounded as if everyone could find a job in California. Dust Bowl families headed west.

BIG NUMBERS

During the 1930s, nearly three million people left the Dust Bowl.

Some people did not have cars or trucks. They loaded a few things into wagons or onto carts and wheelbarrows and started walking down the highway.

On the Road

The Dust Bowl families drove for miles and miles. They slept in their cars or on the side of the road. They washed their clothes and their bodies in streams. They went to the bathroom behind bushes. Sometimes they ate only apples for dinner. They saved the cores for another meal.

This old car broke down on the road. The dad might knock on a farmer's door and offer to paint a fence or pick some cherries. That will give him enough money to fix the car and move on.

NO JOBS

Between 1935 and 1940, more than one million people moved to California. There were too many people and not enough jobs. California had many signs like this one: "If You Are Looking For Work: Keep Out."

There were plenty of farms in California. But soon there were too many workers. Some people found jobs on large farms. They picked grapes, plums, peaches, potatoes, lettuce, or cotton. When the picking was done, the workers had to move.

Farm Camps

Workers who moved from farm to farm were called **migrant workers**. They camped out near the farms where they worked. Some workers lived in tents. Some lived in one-room **shacks** made of cardboard or tin. They slept on the ground and had no bathrooms.

A family of six lived in this homemade shack. Many migrant workers got sick from drinking dirty water and not eating enough food.

Most cabins at the government camps had no kitchens. Cooks made hot meals. The workers bought breakfast for a penny a day.

In 1936, the United States **government** built camps for the migrant workers. Workers paid a dollar a week for a one-room tent or cabin. The camps had hot showers and toilets. Some had a playground, a baseball diamond, and a school.

School

While the Dust Bowl children traveled to California, they did not go to school. Some of them missed many months or even years. When their parents found work in California, the children started at a new school. But they only stayed there for a few months. When their parents' work was done, they had to move.

This is a **migrant worker** and her two children at a **government** camp at Nipomo, California, in 1936. The family lived in a tent.

These children of migrant workers are at Sunday school in a government camp in Marysville, California. A bus took them to school and church.

Many Dust Bowl children had a difficult time at their new schools. They had missed many lessons and could not catch up with the local students. They also were teased for their patched clothing and the way they pronounced their words.

SCHOOL LESSONS

- Arithmetic
- Handwriting
- Reading the Bible
- Good manners
- American history
- Sports and games

Food

People who had no homes sometimes ate in public parks. Some parks had cooking areas where people could build a fire. Someone put a kettle of water on the fire and others brought food to boil. One person might cook a potato. Another might cook a hot dog.

This family lives in a **government** camp cabin. Instead of chairs, this family sits on boxes when eating at the table.

Migrant Worker Recipe – Meat Stew

Here is a recipe you can make on an outdoor grill or in a campfire. If you do not have an outdoor grill or fire, cook the foil packets in an oven at 350 degrees Fahrenheit (180°C).

WARNING: Do not cook anything unless there is an adult to help you. Always ask an adult to cut the food, build the fire, and place and remove food from the hot coals, grill, or oven.

YOU WILL NEED

For each serving:

2 sheets of aluminum foil each 17 inches (42 centimeters) long and 12 inches (30 centimeters) wide
1 washed and sliced potato
1/2 washed and sliced green pepper
1 washed and sliced carrot
1/4 cup (60 ml) chopped onion
1/4 pound (110 g) ground beef or turkey
1 teaspoon butter
salt and pepper

FOLLOW THE STEPS

1. Have an adult start the fire in the grill or campfire. Let the coals burn down until they are glowing red.
2. Place the two pieces of foil on top of each other. Spread some butter on the top sheet of foil.
3. Place one serving of ground meat on top of the butter in the center of the foil. Flatten it to about 1/2 inch (12 mm) thick.
4. Place the sliced potato, pepper, carrot, and onion on the meat.
5. Sprinkle salt, pepper, and the rest of the butter on the vegetables.
6. Wrap the doubled piece of foil over the food. Fold the ends a few times to keep the juices from spilling out.
7. Put the foil packet, folded sides up, on the grill, on the coals, or in the oven. Cook 1 hour.

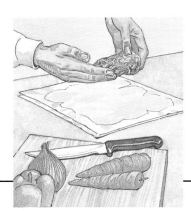

Rain in the Dust Bowl

At last, after seven long years, the clouds opened up over the Dust Bowl. Finally, there were enough rainy days to make the **crops** grow. Farmers who had stayed planted seeds in their fields again. Some farmers came back from California and other places. Others decided to stay away. They had found new jobs, new friends, and new homes.

After the Dust Bowl years, farmers started planting their fields in ways that would keep the rain water in the **soil** and keep the soil from blowing away. Today, the **Great Plains** once again produce huge amounts of grain. Here, grain is being harvested from fields.

Glossary

borrow to use something that belongs to someone else, with permission

crop plant grown for food

drought several months, or longer, without rain

entertainment things to do for fun, such as listening to the radio or watching a movie or a ballgame

government people who make laws and decisions for the people

Great Plains land between the Mississippi River and Rocky Mountains. It is mostly flat or gently rolling land.

migrant worker person who moves around to work jobs as they are needed

mill building where things, such as flour or clothing, are made using the power of wheels driven by wind or flowing water

newsreel short film about what is happening in the world. It was shown at movie theaters before the days of television.

plow farm machine used to turn over the soil before seeds are planted

shack small hut or house made quickly and cheaply

soil dirt or earth in which plants grow

tornado very strong whirling wind and funnel-shaped cloud that moves over the land

tumbleweed bushy plant that dries up and blows around in the wind

More Books to Read

Wroble, Lisa A. *Kids During the Great Depression.* New York: Rosen Publishing Group, 1999.
An older reader can help you read this book:
Stanley, Jerry. *Children of the Dust Bowl: The True Story of the School at Weedpatch Camp.* New York: Crown Books for Young Readers, 1992.

Index